My Little Book of Poems

Mattyrose Williams

CONTENTS

Alone in the Garden

Not an aeroplane to spy
As I stared into the sky
Wondering in the stillness
Sends shivers up my spine

A little red sparrow chirps
A butterfly at the rosebud sucks
A lone bird on the gate perturbed
No one's in sight to be disturbed

The gentle breeze caress my face
Oh, so refreshing, stillness base
alone in the garden carelessly placed
Enjoying the beauty of nature replaced

Oh, where has everyone gone?
Locked up indoors their will be done
Endless moments will be stored
History's bliss will be secured

(March 2020 lockdown)

Victim of Circumstance

No Sense of it
No frame of Reference
No one to shred a light
On Their suffering Plight
The wrath of Corona
Unquestionable took hold
Does not discriminate
But spreads it wings
Through the minority groups
No way to avoid it?
Such fear it inhibits
Can anyone help?
Can't make a statement.
Just watch, sanitise, isolate, and wait

(March 2020 lockdown)

Blast from the Past

Now I'm old and living with my kids
I reminisce on the past
As I want to pay back
All the joys they provided
Growing old and living with my kids

I make much noise
Play my music so loud
Exercise and bob
As I re-live my teens.
Now growing old and living with my kids

I bounce up and down
With a lift so high
And crash gently down
With a soft bang, bang.
Now growing old and living with my kids

They shake their fingers
And raise their heads.
When the music's loud.
But they'll never know the things I did
Before I got this old.

The gardening's done, the baking done
Exercise, and the lot
Now I can't go out, the gate is locked
What else is there to do?
Now growing old and living with my kids

I paint the walls green
Nail photos on the beam
Create this vivid scene
Of moments long being
Now growing old and living with my kids

I make no compromise
For this household confusion
Brought about by corona.
So I'll drink to lockdown
And await the day when Covid shuts down

(April 2020 lockdown)

I'm Still Here

I cannot tell but wish I knew
Where the invisible objects go
Over the horizon sunset bliss
Strewn across the oceans' mist?

Out in the wilderness the victor strays
Looking for natures' replenishing gaze
The amazing expanse of natures' might
Illuminates and distorts the land

Your wilderness is bare
The tormented mind flare
Battered, broken, sunken deep,
Tired, embolden by natures' sleep

Set me loose to comfort the dawn
My twisted mind some comfort seek
Deep down in the valley the sunlight leak
Shedding light upon this soul so weak

I hear the running water flow
Steaming mist as the wind doth blow
My thirsty soul its quench fulfil
Ever thankful, blissful glee

My wilderness glows from every direction
Transformed in the midst of natures' perfection
Released from impediments strangulation
Freedom to grow in every embarkation.

(April 2020 lockdown)

Garbage City

Another world exits
Far away from humanity
It's called Garbage City
Where life is a reality.

Garbage, garbage, everywhere
Smells congest the atmosphere
Narrow streets with lines outstretched
Support the clothes from the windows' ledge
All fighting for space in the murky air
Clothes hanging everywhere.

Animals wonder to and fro
Taking their pick from the garage pile.
Unkempt children happily playing
Oblivious of their circumstance
What chaos and commotion!

Concerns not expressed
As they trod the muddy street
Everyone's about their business
Escaping their fate
As the garbage trucks struggle the path
to claim their narrow space.

Visitors drive pass in awe
Wondering how to snap a pic
Stared eyes upon the stranger fixed
How dare they drive through our city!
Friendly greetings now exchanged
Along the street till the journey ends.

It's a way of life at garbage city
Everything is re-cycled!
People are working earning a living.
So Remember Garbage City
And the smells endured
When you drink from a recycled cup!

(Garbage City, Egypt 2018)

Catcher in the Eye

Up the dusty road lay many
Can't believe just what I've seen
A mighty horse laid on its back
A black dog on its' side aghast
Hot and ridged and covered in dust.
Take your pick, eh flies and dogs
Do not rush! There is enough to
Last many suns to set.

The horses, the camels, in their stately gear
Riding slowly to nowhere, anywhere!
Their luggage, the people, inhaling the air
Oblivious of carcasses in the way
Just passed by slowly on their way
Riding into the unknown.

Up the slope the dogs relaxed
'Are they dead?' a voice hailed out
"No"...replied the caretaker
'I can whistle if you wish'
At the sound the dogs jumped up!
Thank God they are alive
Else more stench would spoil the fun.

The mopeds speedily overtake
Smiling, waving, as they haste
Time to stop and take your pic
Let the stately camel stoop
Then you'll gentle lay your feet
On this blessed sand spread out like sheets
Where our Lord once stood to teach.

The view incredible to behold
From front the bricks sore eyes can see
Behind its desert vastly spread
From east and west to north and south
The three triangles mighty stand
It is the pyramid! Egypt's point
Built by the slaves under Pharaohs' rule.
Bondage, set free through the red sea route.
Still a site for the visiting few.

Rest ye awhile, take in the views
Pillows, and mats, "Here! Stretch if you wish"
Now we are ready to take our leave
From this amazing incredible scene
What an experience! the desert we've seen
To remain in our brain until it no longer being.

(Egypt 2018)

The Little Boy and his Caged Dog

Up the winding path they trod
Singing happily as they jump
Passersby salute and stare
Amazed to see the bond so cute

Tired from school
Still he insists
My dog must be released
Above anything else

I must obey his call
For walks, for food, for cuddles
But I must find time for homework
Else my eye pad gets messed-up

My chores has increase
As my stamina decreases
Shall I send him to London?
Where he will find a friend
Be home with Granny?
Instead of a cage?
I'll ask my Mom

(Egypt 2019)

Stepping Out

Your friends, My friends.
The Noise, the food
The moods, the shout.
The laughter, the cries, the hugs!
I'll miss all these.
Now you are 22
It is time to go
Time has moved on
You've done good for yourself.
I'm so proud of you
Our Home, now a house
Will now be quiet
I'll try birdwatching
As you recommend
So take the big step
Be careful as you step
REMEMBER;
There'll be sunny days
And rainy days
But you'll cope
'Cause of the 'Roots'
Laid down from birth till now.
You'll make it there.

Now you've returned
You've made it there
With bumps and jumps
Your resilience tested
Satan defeated
You endured the storm
But stayed grounded to your roots.
There's time enough
To re-bond with family
As you reminisce on future plans.
Welcome home!
And into lockdown 2022

(A daughter's homecoming)

Mother

Your days were long and dreary
Your nights, they seem no end
The times I get so angry
as your pain took on no end.

In your despair you could not hear
I prayed to God to ease your fear
To give me strength to bear your groan
Afraid I laid and numb with grief.

I ask my Lord what had she done
To suffer such pain, unbearable hell
I've just travelled six thousand miles to repel
I feel sick, I must run! why did I come?

I must find some comfort to cope with her groans
Jesus, he suffered and died for mankind
It's recorded he said, lay your weary soul down
You will not suffer any more than you can endure.

Give me your hand, Mum
Hold tightly in mine
Breathe in and out deeply
And I'll have a cry
Tomorrow is the day
When your op will allow
Your pains and your groans
To disappear without doubt.

You are now free of pain
But I still feel your pain
When on your return
I was afraid to touch you
So frightened, so numb.

With disbelief the nurse repeats
'It is your Mother in a delirious state.'
I wish I was stronger Your pain was mine
There were lots to tell but no time to spare
As you live for your pain
I love you, dear Mother as your weary soul rest
For your endurance my strength now behold

Jubilee Poem

Left, right, left, right!
The head girl repeats
Stand still! Eyes right! Eyes front!
Now relax and wave the Flag.

The sweltering heat soon took its toll
Many subjects fell, as speeches went on.
The Red Cross came and stood them still
Fulfilling duty to crown and Queen.

You reign over us with such skill and gentleness
Bringing cultures together through the Commonwealth list
Your subjects embrace You through thick and thin
Saying God Save our Queen for a reign so bliss.

In your endeavours you carried on
Through wars and conflict your strength upheld
Fulfilling the lifelong promise held
You serve your subjects truly well.

From Coronation to Platinum you serve us well
With true endurance your duty upheld
We obey your commands for empire days
Marching synchronise as the bands played on.

So let us celebrate this glorious Platinum Jubilee
Hail together "God save the Queen'
70 years of service duly filled
A life well spent, a life well lived.

(Jubilee celebration June 2022)

Dreams

Dreams are filled with winter breezes
Rattling sounds through piercing ears
Ever strengthening though unerring
Altering as direction change
Meandering over streams and lakes
Shadows deep beyond the mist

(Lockdown April 2020)

True Love

True Love is like a sweet Red Rose
Resting beneath the ripples of its stalk
Uniting every soul and man
Everlasting Joy and Peace
Lurking its way deep into the soul
Overtly conquering challenges
Ventures on the verge of hate
Eternal Love true empathy embrace

(Lockdown April 2020)

Adoration

Adoration a selfless crush
Dissolves itself in endless bliss
Over hills and mountains hewed
Rest beyond the heartfelt soul
Attest its' strength in various ways
Trusting ever deeply Still
Infinite limitless Love
Omnipotent power executed will
Nurturing loves' enduring strength
(Lockdown April 2020)

Limerick Poem

There was a young man name Wobble
Who spoke to his goats on their travel
When asked what he said
Nanny goat shock her head
And replied, it's nothing but gabble

Wobble moaned his way home
As his old goats let roam
Puzzled and broken to keep them in form
Wishing instead he was occupied and norm
But remained sad and beaten and lone

(Lockdown May 2020)

Limerick Poem

There was a strange man name Vic
Who walked with a hump and a stick
He carried a large clock,
His ego in shock
as he bounced up the stairs with his crick

He soon miss a step when a stranger led drift
but picked up his gate in a swift
When asked what's the time,
He stretched out a smile
Then lashed the poor guy with his stick.

He should've walked with his watch
but carried a clock
He was dumb as a bat,
Could never read time
Yet carried a watch and a clock.

(Lockdown May 2020)

Images of Love

Seeds of love begins with Compassion
Sown across the roots of conception
Builds up abundantly once nurtured in love
Empowered reflecting the images of God.

Like a tree with twisted thorns
The mother baby bond is born
Where does love grow?
But planted in our hearts since birth
Endorsed with Compassion
Grows and nurture with daily prayer
Love and participation.

(Lockdown May 2020)

Kermit the Frog

As I wondered in the garden
Amidst the cloudless skies
Up sprung a lone frog from the pond
staring me with bulging eyes.

Are you looking for a mate
To keep you warm in your embrace
You looked so bruised and unkempt
Or have you lost your way?

I would love to be your friend
Assist you in your lonely spell
Your life of that recluse dispel
Would lure a mate into your cell.

I'm in awe of your beauty
As you hop around slowly
Can I just touch you
Then you can hop along your way?

(December 2022,on a favourite cartoon character)

On Parting

Time well spent is precious
So tarry awhile at Newlans
cherished moments spent together
Will remain in ones' heart forever.

Together for a common goal
The soaring task fulfil
The forest cleared, the fires lit
Then natures' task begins.

In the evening at suppertime
When thoughts and words exchange
Behold the heart warm meeting
Set loose the tensely tone.

Self-satisfied the journey ends
Our spirits lifted high
And everyday will leave us
In thoughts we'll meet again.

Now we are condemned to part
Shared blessings on our way
So there's no use in weeping
But a merry heart for home.

(June 2022 holiday with siblings)

Surreal Dominique

From sun up to sun down
The true spirit is discovered
Wherever your compass takes you
Your trip will be one of a kind

From sulphur spa to mud pools
Waterfalls to natural springs
From mountain climb to a dip in the river
Enjoy the sun wrenched beauty
Of this nature island chill

The early morning showers
Are blessings to the farmers
At eventide the chant of insects unseen
Sets the tone for the approaching night

On this land there are endless possibilities
Hills and valleys untouched, unspoilt
Sea to explore with winds in your sails
Only on this nature filled paradise, Dominica

(A holiday experience, March 2023)

Harvest Poem

Through sweat and toil the seeds are sown
Steered on by Gods' almighty hand
Mother Nature plays her part
Protects the stronger ones to yield.

The year has turned full cycle
As seasons come and go
E'en the crops are growing
Amid the north winds blast.

The colour now high with golden fields
The farmers spirits calm
Rejoicing in their labour
As the autumn gift is poured.

At last the crops are gathered in
Heaped high the farmers pantry store
To feed us when the storms do drift
And fill us with the heavenly bliss.

So open wide the doorway
As Thanksgiving comes again
Celebrate Gods' love with praise
As we present our harvest gifts.

(October 2022)

The Wounds we Carry

It's a long, long winding road
That never wearies many
That Road is called Remembrance
Where the wounds of slavery dwells.
Ancestral wounds buried
deep into the memory cells
Extends beyond boundaries of our skin
Destroys the soul and twist the mind.

Where does this end and healing begins
From this endless repetition of mistakes
sanctified by mankind?
Ours the burden carried through generations.
Only by repentance of the wrongs done through time
By our masters can one free ones' emotional self.

It's like our collective dreaming
We bare each other's burdens and joys
In ways we are not entirely conscious of
How can one forget the impact of the wounds of slavery
When it's all around us
In our History, our Culture, and Heritage.

We must surrender to the pain
Let the tears out, move forward
Our ancestors fought the battle
And fighting for their freedom
We are free.

In a world of today where injustices prevail
Be a Mandela
In a world of today where wokeness
And disingenuousness prevail
Be a Marcus Garvey
In a world of today Be a Harriet Tubman
Speak out on the evils of modern slavery
In a world of today keep learning and
Be your authentic self.

(October 2022)

Diversity and Culture

Tonight we celebrate our love together
Standing as One people with rich cultures
United in drums and dance and singing
Like birds in the morning with hope and passion
Evidence of our ancestral lives, our life
Our way of life.

As I look at the faces around me I see diversity
I have friends from different countries
Listen to the many languages and mother tongues
I'm not familiar with
Diversity raised me to a higher level
To accept my culture even more.

Diversity raised us
Our colourful array of costumes and flags
Portray our culture
But food, Faith, and love
Is what connects us.

Culture and Diversity are gifts from God
Created at the time of the Tower of Babel
So lets' recognise these gifts
And celebrate our uniqueness.

We are all One race
All One of a kind in culture
Maintaining our individual identity
Through celebration of this diversity
Our Life joins us with Happiness.

(November 2022)

Christmas Poem

Christmas always finds its way
No matter what schemes some Nations play
Infectious Joy it brings to all
Lifts the mood with smiles all round

Santa has travelled through North winds with gifts
To remind us all of Our special gift
To open our hearts to loved ones in need
And extend the joy in giving and sharing

Happily around the tree we gather
With flickering lights we open our gifts
Singing carols to express our joy
And celebrate Christ
The Light of the world is born

To save us from our Sins he came
Christians unite! The Anti-Christ is here
Our World is rapidly changing
The Narrative has changed
Many do not know Christ
So remain strong in your faith
The world of God Never changes.

(December 2022)

80th Birthday Poem

Happy Birthday dear Sister
You are a real Triple Moon
That symbol of female strength
And all it represents
Today is your special day
Enjoy it to the fullest
May you feel young at heart and
Don't let age slow you down
Stay healthy and fit for as long as you can
Stay connected to family and friends
Continue to grow closer to them.
Today, dear Sister God has given you
That golden age of 80
After going through a lifetime of struggle
And with so much responsibilities to juggle
We are happy to see you standing strong and tall
Celebrating your 80th year.
A proud moment for us
You are truly blessed

(February 2023)

When we are Tempted

We are put to the test
We must pray for strength to withstand it
As temptation triggers guilt
Satan wants to destroy believers
Through sin, shame, and guilt
Take heed to Gods' words and
Just do as JESUS did
Rely on the word of God and
Stand fast in your commitment
To worship God alone.
We must follow Jesus' example
And stand strong

(ref. Luke 4:1: 13)

28

When we are Uncertain about the Future

As believers, we should turn
To the Bible to experience
The safety and joy it brings
In uncertain times
God holds the future and HE
Has plans for each of us
HE will keep his promise
And do what's best for our future
Put your trust in him as Abram did.
Gods' blessings are beyond
Our imagination.

(Genesis 15 1-12, 17-18)

When I'm lost

I struggle to find my way
I pray to God to help me
And HE came to rescue me
HE taught me about Repentance
HE taught me about Forgiveness
Following where HE leads me
My life direction changed
Then I realised it was not
A bad thing to be lost
For I began to understand myself
One can never out-sin
Gods' forgiveness
The love of our heavenly father is unconditional.
So too is the fathers' love for his prodigal son.

(ref. Luke 15: 11:3)

The Servant Leader

'DO YOU KNOW WHAT I HAVE DONE FOR YOU?'
Jesus taught His disciples about His kingdom
He washed their feet
A lowly task for a slave
He showed the greatest is the least
His act exemplifies humility and kindness
He anointed their feet
Gave them the power
Sends them out in humility and love to serve
As followers of Jesus we should use
Humility in our relationship with others
Look on with favour to those who are humbly
Jesus came to serve and humble Himself in everything
So we must wash one another's feet
'If I have washed your feet'
Do something to help your neighbour
If the Lord can do it, You can do it.

(Ref. John 13:1-7)

Holy Wednesday

Judas the Traitor
made a deal
For thirty pieces of silver
The deal was sealed
He kissed his friend as promised
On Friday
To identify him to the Sanhedrin

How could a friend so close to Jesus
Suddenly turn away!
Sin is always in the heart
Betrayal started with Judas first
Betrayal teaches us how to avoid turning away from Jesus

Maundy Thursday

At HIS last supper on that Thursday night
Jesus took bread, broke it and shared it around
They all drank from a cup of red wine
He gave a new commandment
To love one another
The broken bread would remind them of his broken body
The wine would remind them of his blood
when he died on the cross
Christians believe bread and wine
Are symbols of the body and blood of Jesus
Taking part in the breaking of bread service
Helps us to remember Jesus and his death
Upon the cross
As believers, our salvation comes through Christ
And the sacrifice of His body upon the cross

By His Stripes we are Healed

Good Friday Poem

HE bled for us!
He bled for us!
He died for our sins
Flogged and lashed by the Roman whip
To a sacrificial death upon the cross.
He bore our sins in HIS body
That we might die to sin and live to righteousness
Such suffering encountered, and yet forgive!

HE paid the price and believers are free
Though blameless, Perfect and sinless was HE
HIS punishment was huge!
It brought us peace and by HIS wounds (stripes)
we are (spiritually) healed
We are forgiven and
We are saved.

(Ref. Isaiah 53:v 5)

Eastertime

Blossom by blossom the Spring time begins
Forewarns the time of rebirth is near
The dark winter days are no longer with us
The sun rising from the East
Points to the Spirit of New beginnings
The sun setting in the west
Reflects the brightness of creation
Like fire upon the horizon

Life comes alive! It is joyous
We have been granted a second chance
Permission is given to leave old lives behind
Focus on the new day with all its potential for joy
And choices that honour God

We all enjoy our Easter eggs
That ancient symbol of fertility
Millions are spent on these eggs each year
And children partake the egg searching game
the hide and seek way
All in celebration of the resurrected Christ

Christians Celebrate!
It is Easter Sunday
Our Sabbath
Christ has risen
The Resurrection proves it
Jesus is the Christ (Messiah) and the son of God
Everything HE said and did was true
Now is the time for renewal of faith

(March 2023)

Mothering Sunday

Mothers, foster Mothers, Mother figures
Come! This is our day
Our one free day of the year
To be blessed for just rewards
As our children gather to tell us and show us
How much they love us
How much they care
for the million things we've given them
To steer them on their way.

A bunch of flowers or chocolate
Won't go amiss
We are blessed to call you
'our daughter, our son'
And we love you too.

Our love for them is an enduring love
a love that no one can explain
And a wondrous evidence of
Gods' tender guiding hands.

So let us celebrate together
This Mothering Sunday with joyfulness
And thanksgiving to
To all Mothers everywhere.

(March 2023)

King Charles *III*

The day of Coronation has dawned
The Spring Sun is clouded
The streets are decorated with Banners
and Flags
To honour a man born to be King.

Laughter and tears
Like us He has known and
His Flaws put to the test
Whether right or wrong
Regal respect is truly recognised
In our country rooted in traditions

Emotive days, no doubt he'll have
As He ascends the throne
Pray, God grant him wisdom like king Solomon
To serve and guide His people.

A new Era has begun.
Welcome to the throne King Charles
His Coronation is all OUR story.
6th May '23

My Little Book of Poems is dedicated to my mother, Matilda

whose passing first inspired me to write poems.

Her spirit is interwoven in some of these narratives.

My themes span events, places,

people, nature, family and religion, to name a few.

I try to keep an emotional connection to all these things and

would like to share my poems with others.

Printed in Great Britain
by Amazon

32396413R00030